BURNING QUESTIONS

Burning Questions

A resource for evangelism

PAUL FIELD *and* STEPHEN DEAL

Conceived and co-ordinated by Rob Frost

KINGSWAY PUBLICATIONS

EASTBOURNE

Biblical quotations are taken from the Good News Bible
© American Bible Society 1976.

ISBN 0 85476 448 8

Produced by Bookprint Creative Services
P.O. Box 827, BN23 6NX, England for
KINGSWAY PUBLICATIONS LTD
Lottbridge Drove, Eastbourne, E. Sussex BN23 6NT.
Printed in Great Britain

Contents

Introduction 7

1. What's gone wrong with the world? 11

2. Can I start again, please? 21

3. What's the point of it all? 29

4. What's the cost of becoming a Christian? 31

5. Could God use someone like me? 41

6. How do I become a Christian? 49

7. Is there life after death? 59

8. Can I know Jesus? 67

The 'On fire' song 79

Contents

INTRODUCTION

Imagine the scene. The church is packed. The last chords of a hymn die away, and the congregation sits down. The minister stands and announces that the newly-formed drama group is going to perform. Four people tiptoe nervously on to the slightly raised area behind the communion rail.

'Are you ready?' whispers one.

'Go on, you start.'

There is a long pause. The congregation begin to shuffle uncomfortably.

'Oh, it's me!' giggles one of the group, and launches into his first line.

The sketch that should have lasted three minutes drags on for five (though it feels more like twenty-five). Was one of the characters meant to have a bad cold, or had the actor just forgotten to blow his nose? The sketch may have had something to do with a parable, but you are not quite sure which one, because two of the cast couldn't be heard, and most of the rather confusing mime (why *were* they washing an elephant with a lawn mower?) took place behind a pillar.

If this is your experience of drama in church then here is an opportunity to restore its reputation as an effective means of communicating the gospel. Here are sketches that have been tried and tested in front of real audiences. Most require only a little space, and do not assume the performing area has ideal sight lines from all parts of the church or hall. Props and costume can be kept to an absolute minimum, or you can be as creative as you wish.

Christians often find it difficult to find a way in to witnessing. The resources in this book provide the kind of contact which opens up conversation and sharing naturally and spontaneously, and in a non-threatening way. The project is designed to make the Christian faith approachable and user friendly, and to demonstrate that being a Christian is not only a serious matter, but also lots of fun!

Drama and music are the vernacular of our generation. People receive many of their messages about society and the world through pop music or 'soaps', and the church must learn how to speak this language and how to communicate in it as simply and dramatically as Jesus did in his generation.

The music and drama in this presentation cannot answer all the burning questions which people ask, but they are designed to introduce people to Jesus and to an understanding of his love for them.

The whole presentation lasts for about an hour, but some churches and youth groups may not be able to tackle the entire package. Look carefully at the different aspects and select which parts can be done well by your own group.

There are two ways of using the production:

1. Cabaret style

At a community event where many non-Christians are present one or two sections could be used followed by a short testimony. The mission team, sitting around tables, chat with visitors, picking up on their reactions to the different pieces by using the trigger questions as part of the conversation. There should be quite long gaps between items to allow conversations to develop.

2. Guest service style

Use sections of the presentation interspersed with brief testimonies which answer the trigger questions listed. It may not be necessary to illustrate all the sections with testimony, though a good speaker may care to elaborate on some of the themes for a moment or two.

The evening should be tied together by a brief talk after the Saul drama, and the Burning Questions song used as an opportunity for response. Inviting people forward to take a copy of John's gospel is an effective way of identifying those who may be searching for answers.

Preparation

While groups should aim to present this material to professional standard, it is important that rehearsals are also times for fellowship, prayer and enjoyment. If you don't enjoy yourselves, it is unlikely that your audience will!

Each section ideally requires three rehearsals. The first should be spent reading through the piece and blocking it – that is, working out all the essential movements, entrances and exits. All necessary props should be identified at this stage. A suitable gap should be left between the first and second rehearsal to allow for the learning of lines, the gathering of props and the practice of the music.

By the end of the second rehearsal people should really feel that they know what they are doing. Someone who is not actually performing should watch at this stage and make constructive criticisms. Ask the following questions: Will the audience be able to hear everything? Will they be able to see everything? Does everyone know their lines?

The third rehearsal should be very short and as close to the performance as possible. Ideally it should take place in the actual venue. Make sure you can have access to the performing area with the minimum of distraction to the audience, and that the space is clear. If you are using microphones or any other technical paraphernalia now is the time to check that everything is working.

Preparation and rehearsal times can also be opportunities for training in evangelism. It would be good if each member of the team knew how to share their testimony by the end of rehearsals. The group could be joined by others willing to become part of the witness team accompanying the actors and musicians, and the whole group should read the Bible passages suggested and understand the purpose of each section.

Remember that prayer is the key to effective mission. Make prayer together an important priority at each rehearsal – and before every presentation.

Once the presentation is rehearsed to a good standard, why not take it round schools, colleges, pubs, clubs, youth centres and parks near you? We did a mission in fifteen British nightclubs on the Costa Brava, and it was a fantastic opportunity to share and to witness.

Remember, you don't have to perform the entire eight sections. Just do what feels good to you.

And do write and let us know how you get on!

Rob Frost and his team are based at Raynes Park Methodist Church, Tolverne Road, London SW20 8RA.

What's gone wrong with the world?

CONVERSATION STARTER: What do *you* think has gone wrong
with the world?

MUSIC: Long way back to Eden.

DRAMA: Would you Adam and Eve it?

MUSIC REPRISE

Most people today recognise that the world is in a terrible mess. Pollution, mass starvation, the threat of global warfare, religious and political persecution and ethnic cleansing are just a few of the symptoms of the world's brokenness.

Christians believe that when God created the world it was perfect. It is through human sinfulness and selfishness that the world has been spoiled, but God has prepared a 'way back to Eden'.

Use this drama/music sequence to ask people what they think is wrong with the world . . . and why it's in the state it is.

Genesis 3:17-23 explains the Fall, and Romans 5:12-25 and 1 Corinthians 15:20-22 explain how, though death came into the world through disobedience, there is a way back to the peace and joy of Eden for each individual through the death and resurrection of Jesus.

Note the key words in the reprise following the drama: 'There's a road laid by God's own tears . . .'.

LONG WAY BACK TO EDEN

Paul Field

Brightly

It's a long way to E - den from here,— to find a

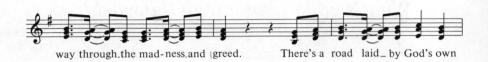

way through the mad-ness and |greed. There's a road laid— by God's own

tears; it's a long— way back to E - den from here.—

Piano

Verse

1. Long a - go— when all — the world— was new,—
2. Tempt-ed by— the fruit— of |our— de - sire, we

ev' - ry - thing was beau - ti - ful and bright. a
on - ly hear the things we want to hear;

Some-where on the way it broke in two, di -
con science kept in chains be - hind the wire,

vi - ded by our choice of wrong and right. We
hos - tage to the for - tune and the fear.

tra - ded in our in no - cence to tra - vel on our own, now we
Dri - ven by our self - ish - ness, we try to run the game, now there's

can't find our way home. It's a
no - one else to blame.

Chorus
(3rd time instrumental)

long way to E - den from here; to find a
way through the mad - ness and greed. There's a
road laid by God's own tears; it's a long

14

15

LONG WAY BACK TO EDEN (REPRISE)

Paul Field

It's a long way— to E - den from here; — to find a

way through—the mad - ness— and greed. There's a

road laid — by God's own tears; it's a long—

way back to E - den from here. ___ It's a long ___

___ way back to E - den from here. ___ It's a

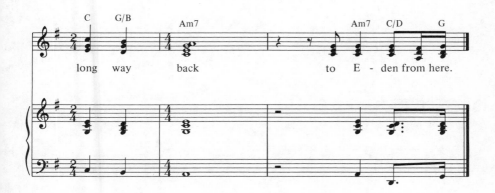

long way back to E - den from here.

17

It's a long way to Eden from here,
To find a way through the madness and greed.
There's a road laid by God's own tears:
It's a long way back to Eden from here.

Long ago when all the world was new,
Everything was beautiful and bright.
Somewhere on the way it broke in two,
Divided by our choice of wrong and right.
We traded in our innocence to travel on our own,
Now we can't find our way home.

It's a long way to Eden from here,
To find a way through the madness and greed.
There's a road laid by God's own tears:
It's a long way back to Eden from here.

Tempted by the fruit of our desire,
We only hear the things we want to hear.
A conscience kept in chains behind the wire,
Hostage to the fortune and the fear.
Driven by our selfishness we try to run the game –
There's no one else to blame.

It's a long way to Eden from here,
To find a way through the madness and greed.
There's a road laid by God's own tears:
It's a long way back to Eden from here.

Would you Adam and Eve it?

ADAM and EVE are standing behind a small shrub.

ADAM: What's it all about? I ask you!

EVE: What are you whining on about now, Adam?

ADAM: One moment we're in the garden of Eden, paradise. The next we're stuck out here and the whole place is covered in weeds. And all because of one stupid bit of fruit.

EVE: Oh don't bring that up again. I've said I'm sorry.

ADAM: A whole blooming garden of fresh produce and you have to pick the one piece of forbidden vegetable matter. Why didn't you give me some passion fruit? I love passion fruit.

EVE: It wasn't my fault.

ADAM: Oh yes. That's another thing. Why did you listen to a snake? A snake! I ask you. You never listen to me.

EVE: He was very persuasive.

ADAM: He's a snake! How can a snake be persuasive?

eve: Well, he was so charming. He told me that if you and I ate the fruit of that particular tree we could gain wisdom.

ADAM: And you believed him.

EVE: He seemed so wide eyed and innocent.

ADAM: Wide eyed and innocent! Of course he was wide eyed – he's a snake. He hasn't got any eyelids. And if I ever get my hands on him he won't have any legs either.

EVE: Violence isn't the answer.

ADAM: Oh yes? You tell that to the lion. He's just eaten three sheep. The whole world's gone crazy, I tell you.

EVE: It's not my fault.

ADAM: Well, it certainly isn't mine. I was perfectly happy pottering around doing a bit of pruning and naming the animals.

EVE: Well, that's just the point, isn't it? You were never there. But you expected me to get the supper. If you did your

19

	share of work around the house instead of leaving it all to me perhaps none of this would have happened.
ADAM:	Don't go shifting the blame on to me. I've been working flat out trying to find a name for that horse with the black and white stripes.
EVE:	You'll have to start using another letter.
ADAM:	I've only got one left. Everything is running down and wearing out.
EVE:	I know. This is the third set of fig leaves I've had to find this week.
ADAM:	I keep snagging mine on brambles and things.
EVE:	Doesn't that hurt?
ADAM:	My eyes have been watering all day. I'm sick and tired of it all. Everything used to be so perfect but now it's all in shreds.
EVE:	Quite literally, I see.
ADAM:	Pick me another leaf, will you?
EVE:	Do it yourself. I'm not your servant.
ADAM:	You're so moody these days.
EVE:	You leave my moods out of it.
ADAM:	I don't know what's got into you.
EVE:	Men!
ADAM:	What do you mean men? There's only one of me.
EVE:	Man! then.
ADAM:	You know what I really want? I wish we could start all over again.
EVE:	Well, we can't. We have to pay the price for being disobedient.
ADAM:	We!
EVE:	I'm sorry – I know you are going to blame me for ever but there's nothing we can do about it.
ADAM:	It's God I blame. He's the one who gave us free will and intelligence. He's the one who made us with the ability to mess up. He's the one who should find a way to make it all right again.
EVE:	And how is he going to do that?
ADAM:	I don't know, but he should. Whatever it takes, whatever the cost.
EVE:	Well, there's no point whinging on.
ADAM:	I'm ravenous. How about roasting another unicorn?
EVE:	No, we finished the last of those on Friday. There's some apple pie left.
ADAM:	No, I fancy something roasted. I wonder what that black and white horse tastes like.

Can I start again, please?

> **CONVERSATION STARTER:** Have you any regrets about the way you've lived your life?
>
> **DRAMA:** Short Change.
>
> **MUSIC:** Never too late.

Read the story of Zacchaeus in Luke 19:1-10. Zacchaeus was a traitor. He was deceitful, dishonest and disloyal. As well as working for the Roman occupation force he was making dishonest tax demands. But when he met Jesus his life changed, and he wanted to return the money he'd stolen, and to help the poor.

No matter what we have done, or how badly we feel we've messed up our lives, God loves each of us, and like Zacchaeus, we are given the opportunity to be born again. We can start a fresh life with Jesus as our Lord and friend.

Use this drama and song to talk about personal failure and the way that Jesus Christ offers us all the opportunity to receive salvation in the way that Zacchaeus did.

The wonderful passage in John's gospel about God's great love for us and the need for new birth is found in John 3:1-17. The Christian message is that, as the song says, 'It's never too late for turning a life around.'

Short Change

The sketch takes place in the local branch of a bank. There is scope for any number of non-speaking parts forming a queue behind Zacchaeus.

BEVERLY: Next please! Yes sir, my name is Beverly. How may I be of assistance?

ZACCHAEUS: I'd like to withdraw some money.

BEVERLY: Certainly sir. What name is it?

ZACCHAEUS: Zacchaeus.

BEVERLY: And do you have your account details?

ZACCHAEUS: No. I'm afraid I don't. I came out in rather a hurry.

BEVERLY: I'll have to ask you to fill out one of these green forms . . .

ZACCHAEUS: Fine.

BEVERLY: . . . which will authorise me to allow you to fill out a pink form . . .

ZACCHAEUS: Oh.

BEVERLY: . . . and if you sign here, here, and here . . .

ZACCHAEUS: Right.

BEVERLY: . . . and can you initial it to show me you've signed.

ZACCHAEUS: Er . . . right.

BEVERLY: Now, do you have any identification?

ZACCHAEUS: Not really.

BEVERLY: That presents me with a bit of a problem. You'll have to fill out an orange form.

ZACCHAEUS: Are we working our way through the rainbow?

BEVERLY: Oh very droll, sir. How much would you like to withdraw?

ZACCHAEUS: All of it. Every penny.

BEVERLY: I see. Going on holiday are we, sir? Anywhere nice?

ZACCHAEUS: No. I'm staying here in Jericho.

BEVERLY: Very wise. I get camel-sick myself. Is Sir going to invest the money?

ZACCHAEUS: In a manner of speaking. I'm going to give to the poor and to the people I stole it from.

BEVERLY: Do they give a high rate of interest?

ZACCHAEUS: It's a long-term investment.

BEVERLY: How long?

ZACCHAEUS: Eternal.

BEVERLY: Lovely. Trying to avoid the tax man, are you?

ZACCHAEUS: Not really.

BEVERLY: Not that I blame you. My local tax collector's really horrible. He looks a bit like you actually.

ZACCHAEUS: But a man can change, can't he? He can start again.

BEVERLY: You sound just like that Jesus. He's been going around saying people can change and start all over again. Being born again he calls it.

ZACCHAEUS: Exactly! That's what he told me when he came to my house for tea.

BEVERLY: Jesus went to tea at your house, did he? Lovely. My mum went on a picnic with him. I hope you gave him more than bread and fish.

ZACCHAEUS: I gave him my life.

BEVERLY: Lovely. How do you want your money?

ZACCHAEUS: Cash, please.

BEVERLY: *[She hands over a large sum of money.]* You be careful carrying this amount of money around with you. There are some very strange people about.

ZACCHAEUS: So I've noticed.

BEVERLY: Do you know what? My mum, yesterday morning, opened her bedroom curtains, and there was a man right outside the window. Sat up in a tree he was. Next please!

NEVER TOO LATE

Paul Field

1. So ma-ny things to hold you back, so ma - ny ties that bind.
2. God knows all your hopes and dreams, He knows your doubts and fears.

So ma - ny fears for the fu - ture a - head, and re -
He knows the joy that your laugh - ter can mean, and He

grets for the past be - hind.___ It's hard to be - gin_ to be - lieve_
knows_ your se - cret fears.___ (3.) No mat-ter what_ your past_

___ it's true,___ it's like reach - ing for___ the moon.___ But
___ may hold, of His love He free - ly gives; ___

His love is pain - ting the co - lours in - to___ life's black and white car - toon.
love that for ev - er has bro - ken the mould_ so we may learn to live.___

Chorus

___ Start a - gain, _____ it's nev - er too late ___ for
___ gain, _____ it's nev - er too late, ___

turn - ing a life _ a - round, _ in our weak-ness we are
no mat-ter where_you go, _____ love is al - ways just a

all but lost, be - cause of His love_we are found, _ to |start a -
prayer a - way, it's nev - er too late to let go_

2.

_ and start a - gain.

And

So many things to hold you back, so many ties that bind;
So many fears for the future ahead,
And regrets for the past behind.
It's hard to begin to believe it's true, it's like reaching for the moon;
But this love is painting the colours into life's black and white
cartoon.

Start again. It's never too late for turning a life around.
In our weakness we are all but lost, because of his love we are
found.
To start again, it's never too late, no matter where you go;
Love is always just a prayer away.
It's never too late to let go and start again.

God knows all your hopes and dreams, he knows your doubts and
fears;
He knows the joy that your laughter can mean,
And he knows your secret tears.
No matter what your past may hold of his love he freely gives;
Love that for ever has broken the mould, so we may learn to live.

Start again. It's never too late, for turning a life around.
In our weakness we are all but lost, because of his love we are
found.
To start again, it's never too late, no matter where you go;
Love is always just a prayer away.
It's never too late to let go and start again.

What's the point of it all?

CONVERSATION STARTER: How important to you are the things that you own?

MUSIC: Old McDonald.

Many people spend their lives earning, saving and accumulating things, yet they still often feel dissatisfied. Material possessions do not satisfy the spiritual side of our nature.

This section sets the story of the Rich Fool to the well-known fun song. Read the story, found in Luke 12:13-21, and also study the following section about 'things that last' from Luke 12:22-34.

It's good to ask people about their aims and goals in life, and to measure them by the teaching found in Luke 12. Many people rarely stop to ask whether they are rich in eternal terms.

Jesus said: 'Provide for yourselves purses that don't wear out, and save your riches in heaven, where they will never decrease, because no thief can get to them, and no moth can destroy them. For your heart will always be where your riches are' (Lk 12:33-34).

Old McDonald built a barn – e i e i o,
To store the crops grown on his farm – e i e i o.
With a store it up here, and a store it up there,
Store it up, store it up, everybody store it up.
Old McDonald built a barn – e i e i o.

Soon his business did so well – e i e i o;
He grew more crops than he could sell – e i e i o.
With a store it up here, and a store it up there,
Store it up, store it up, everybody store it up.
Old McDonald built a barn – e i e i o.

When no one could get in the door – e i e i o,
The builders came to build ten more – e i e i o.
With a store it up here, and a store it up there,
Store it up, store it up, everybody store it up.
Old McDonald built a barn – e i e i o.

He felt secure to see the place – e i e i o,
A million tons there 'just in case' – e i e i o.
With a store it up here, and a store it up there,
Store it up, store it up, everybody store it up.
Old McDonald built a barn – e i e i o.

While out one day to harvest more – e i e i o,
He did not hear the tractor's roar – e i e i o.
With a chop it up here, and a chop it up there,
Chop it up, chop it up, everybody chop it up.
Old McDonald came to harm – e i e i o.

He fell beneath the combine's blades – e i e i o,
Now he's chopped and baled and stored away – e i e i o.
With a store it up here, and a store it up there,
Store it up, store it up, everybody store it up.
Old McDonald built a barn – e i e i o.

The moral of this tale of woe – e i e i o,
Is you can't take it with you when you go – e i e i o.
With a store it up here, and a store it up there,
Store it up, store it up, everybody store it up.
Old McDonald built a barn – e i e i o.

What's the cost of becoming a Christian?

CONVERSATION STARTER: What are your highest priorities in life?

DRAMA: The Cost of Living.

MUSIC: Nothing less than everything.

The story of the rich young man which we read in Luke 19:18-30 is a story about priorities. In the end, he went away feeling sad because he wasn't willing to make God's kingdom the highest priority in his life.

The drama, and the song 'Nothing less than everything', pinpoint the fact that there is a high cost involved in following Jesus. It is not something to be done lightly.

In Matthew 10:38-39 we read: 'Whoever does not take up his cross and follow in my steps is not fit to be my disciple. Whoever tries to gain his own life will lose it: but whoever loses his life for my sake will gain it.'

It is in leaving self behind and following him that we discover the joy and liberty of the children of God.

The Cost of Living

DOMINIC:	Ah! My three closest friends. Thank you for coming so swiftly. Clarissa, my darling fiancée. Nanny, dear Nanny. And Harris, my trusty manservant.
HARRIS:	You rang, sir?
DOMINIC:	Indeed I did.
HARRIS:	A matter of some import I would surmise.
DOMINIC:	Absolutely! You would surmise correctly. I have some tremendous news.
CLARISSA:	Oh darling! Are we going to set the day?
NANNY:	Congratulations, Master Dominic.
DOMINIC:	No, no, nothing like that. I've met someone.
CLARISSA:	Oh Dominic!
DOMINIC:	No, not another woman, my little wufferly-pufferly. I've met a Ray-bee.
HARRIS:	A rabbi, sir.
CLARISSA:	But isn't that some kind of holy man?
DOMINIC:	You are exactly right, old thing. He is indeed a holy man. He used to be a carpenter but now he goes about healing people and preaching and . . . and being holy. Jolly exciting, what?
HARRIS:	Would I be correct in presuming that the holy gentleman to whom you are referring is Mr Jesus of Nazareth?
DOMINIC:	You've heard of him!
HARRIS:	Yes, sir. The gentleman seems to have raised a few eyebrows.
DOMINIC:	How so?
HARRIS:	He advocates a personal salvation scheme based on a personal knowledge of himself.
DOMINIC:	Does he, by jove?
HARRIS:	It is deemed somewhat controversial by the religious establishment.

DOMINIC: Oh. Well, I met him earlier today and I asked him what I must do to inherit eternal life.

CLARISSA: What did he say?

DOMINIC: Keep the commandments.

NANNY: You already do that. You were brought up to be a good boy.

CLARISSA: Is that all?

DOMINIC: Just about. Apart from selling everything and giving the proceeds to the poor, and then simply following him.

NANNY: Oh, that's interesting, dear.

DOMINIC: Yes. From now on it's a life on the open road for me. And for you, since I know you'll all be keen to join me.

HARRIS: Join you, sir?

DOMINIC: Of course. I'm going to become a disciple of Mr Jesus. I'm going to give up everything and put my faith in him.

CLARISSA: When you say 'give up everything', what exactly do you mean?

DOMINIC: The business, the estate, the cars. You know, all the unimportant things in life.

CLARISSA: And you want us to join you?

DOMINIC: It'll be a real wheeze. Open air, good companions, doing good, and of course, eternal life. I want all of you to come along and share in it. Lend a hand and what-have-you.

HARRIS: Will this be a salaried position, sir?

DOMINIC: Money isn't the issue, Harris.

HARRIS: That may be the case, sir, but its absence does give rise to certain difficulties.

DOMINIC: How so?

HARRIS: The one that immediately springs to mind, sir, is how precisely, without the prerequisite financial facilities, you plan to retain my services.

CLARISSA: And how do you possibly expect to keep me in the manner to which I've become accustomed?

NANNY: And all that fresh air is only going to bring on your chest again. Especially if you don't keep warm at night.

HARRIS: If I may be so bold as to make a suggestion, sir?

DOMINIC: Er . . . yes. Fire away.

HARRIS: Contact Mr Jesus and ask if you can negotiate for eternal life on more favourable terms.

NANNY: Oh now that is a sensible idea.

CLARISSA: After all, giving up everything for this Jesus fellow is all very well, but you have such an awful lot to give up. Me, for example.

DOMINIC: I have rather, haven't I?

NANNY: Why don't you tell him about your chest. I'm sure he'll understand you need to be kept comfortable.

HARRIS: Explain to him that you were not raised in a manner that prepared you for a life of sacrifice. Tell him you will be happy to make regular donations to a charity of his choice.

CLARISSA: Make him understand that you have responsibilities. Say you'll be happy to give up one day a week for him. Sunday's good. Most of the shops are shut.

DOMINIC: Yes, right. Perhaps I ought to talk to him.

ALL: Yes.

DOMINIC: Right. Let me see . . . *[He takes out a mobile phone.]* He's on Bethany 178. It's ringing . . . Hello? Martha, is Jesus there? Lord? Hello, it's me, Dominic. I'm very well, thank you. Now about this eternal life thing. How much would you say it was *really* worth?

NOTHING LESS THAN EVERYTHING

Paul Field

35

3rd time to Coda ⊕

Verse

what You gave for me, ___ now it's no - thing less than ev' - ry - thing for You.

1. Fi - nal ly ___ I see ___ the place I want to be, ___ I read the wel - come in my Sa - viour's ___
2. You can nev - er put a price ___ on love and sa - cri - fice, ___ You can nev - er count the cost that Je - sus ___

36

eyes. Fi - nal - ly I've found_ my
paid. All the trea - sure on_ the earth_ can't

feet on so - lid ground,_ u - pon a love_that knows_no com-pro-mise._
mea-sure out the worth of a love that will_ be faith - ful all the way._

CODA

No - thing less._
(Ev' - ry - thing.)
No thing less._
(Ev' - ry - thing. ____)

No - thing less_than ev' ry thing._
(Ev'-ry - thing. ____)
No-thing less_than ev'-ry-thing.

37

(Ev' - ry - thing...)

(Tacet)

No - thing less_ than ev' - ry - thing is

how it has_to be; — no - thing less_than ev'-ry-thing will do.

No|thing less_than ev' - ry - thing is what You gave_for me, — now it's
No|thing less_than ev' - ry - thing is what You gave_for me, — now it's

no - thing |less_than ev' - ry - thing for You.
no|thing less_than ev' - ry - thing for You.

No-thing less.

38

Nothing less than everything is how it has to be,
Nothing less than everything will do.
Nothing less than everything is what you gave for me,
Now it's nothing less than everything for you.

Finally I see the place I want to be,
I read the welcome in my Saviour's eyes.
Finally I've found my feet on solid ground,
Upon a love that knows no compromise.

Nothing less than everything is how it has to be,
Nothing less than everything will do.
Nothing less than everything is what you gave for me,
Now it's nothing less than everything for you.

You can never put a price on love and sacrifice,
You can never count the cost that Jesus paid.
All the treasure on the earth can't measure out the worth
Of a love that will be faithful all the way.

Nothing less than everything is how it has to be,
Nothing less than everything will do.
Nothing less than everything is what you gave for me,
Now it's nothing less than everything for you.

Could God use someone like me?

CONVERSATION STARTER: How would you feel about becoming
a Christian?

MONOLOGUE: The Witness for the Prosecution.

MUSIC: Stony Ground

Many people feel that they aren't good enough to become Christians, or that they wouldn't be able to live up to the high standards which are a part of the Christian lifestyle.

The story of Peter's denial, found in John 13:36-38, John 18:15-18 and 25-27, reminds us just how human his disciples were. They knew what it was to fail the Lord . . . and they must have often felt that they weren't worthy to build his kingdom.

Following Jesus is all about recognising our unworthiness, our failure and our weakness, and allowing him to change us day by day into his likeness.

The conversation between Peter and Jesus in John 21:15-19 gives hope to us all.

The Witness for the Prosecution

My name is Tamar.

I'm a servant in the house of Caiaphas.

I was carrying sticks from the woodpile to the fire. It was cool that night, cold even. A few minutes earlier soldiers had brought Jesus into the house. After they had passed through and things had quietened down I saw Simon Peter slip quietly into the courtyard.

Anyone could have seen his distress. Caiaphas was no friend of Jesus, nor of any associated with him. If they could come at night and try the Nazarene, then the rule of law had been put aside, at least on this occasion.

I recognised Simon Peter, as would half Jerusalem at that time. For wherever Jesus was, he was there, loud and assured. He seemed so proud that Jesus had chosen him.

I heard later that when Jesus was arrested Simon Peter defended him with a sword. That was easy to believe.

Yes, I recognised him, he had a certain notoriety. I was young and he was attractive.

By this time several people had gathered around the fire, and when I added wood to its flames I spoke to Simon Peter. I wanted to know what was happening. 'You were with Jesus of Galilee,' I said to him. But he denied it. He said he didn't know what I was talking about. He stood up and walked to the gates of the courtyard. I could see he was shaking.

Naomi, another servant, told those around the fire that she was sure he had been with Jesus. Simon Peter heard her and although he swore before us all that he didn't know him, it was his eyes: his eyes betrayed him.

Eventually one of the men called out loudly that he *knew* he was a follower of the rabbi from Galilee – his accent had given him away. And then in Peter's face I saw panic. There were soldiers all around.

'I swear I'm telling the truth!' he shouted. Everyone turned and looked. 'May God punish me if I am not! I do not know the man!'

At that moment a cock crowed, and for a few seconds there was only silence. Then the soldiers led Jesus from the house. He looked over to where Peter was standing. And in that moment, as they saw each other, caught in the light of the fire, I could see the tears on Peter's face.

Then Peter turned and fled.

STONY GROUND

Paul Field

1. Sure-ly this＿ is sto - ny ground＿ on which to build＿ a
2. Sure-ly this＿ is clou-dy wa-ter for turn-ing in - to

king-dom. ＿＿
wine.

Sure-ly, Lord, You might have＿found＿
Sure-ly the＿most sour and bit-ter

a bet-ter man than me.
of all the grapes up-on Your vine.

There must be ma-ny, Lord, much
Oh, I don't mean to sound un-

wor - thi - er than I, _____
grate - ful, Lord, You know, _

there must be ma - ny, Lord, more
but ev - en with the strength I've

brave, _____ 'cause I fear that I'm not strong e - nough to lift Your cross on
found _____ in all Your pow'r and wis-dom, Lord, there must be some mis -

high.
take;

There must be ma - ny
for I am weak, Lord,

much more wor - thy,
so ve - ry weak, Lord,

ma-ny stron-ger You could save.
and I will on - ly let You down.

Sure-ly this-is sto-

- ny ground,_ my Lord,_ on which to build_ a king - dom. ____

Sure-ly, Lord,You might have found_ a fir-mer rock_than

_ me. ____

For I am weak, Lord, so |ve-ry weak, Lord, and I will on - ly let You, ___ let You down. ___

Surely this is stony ground
On which to build a kingdom.
Surely, Lord, you might have found
A better man than me.
There must be many, Lord, much worthier than I;
There must be many, Lord, more brave.
Cos' I fear that I'm not strong enough to lift your cross up high.
There must be many much more worthy,
Many stronger you could save.

Surely this is cloudy water
For turning into wine.
Surely the most sour and bitter
Of all the grapes upon your vine.
Oh I don't mean to sound ungrateful, Lord, you know,
But even with the strength I've found
In all your power and wisdom, Lord, there must be some mistake.
For I am weak, Lord, so very weak, Lord,
And I will only let you down.

Surely this is stony ground
On which to build a kingdom.
Surely, Lord, you might have found
A firmer rock than me.

How do I become a Christian?

CONVERSATION STARTER: Would you like to become a
Christian?

DRAMA: Thieves' Paradise.

MUSIC: Forgiven.

The story of the dying thief found in Luke 23:26-43 reminds us that it is
never too late to accept Jesus Christ as our Saviour. The thief on the cross
beside Jesus was near to death . . . yet he put his faith in the Lord and heard
Jesus say, 'I promise you that today you will be in Paradise with me' (Lk
23:43).

The thief could not earn his way into heaven, or demonstrate a good
enough lifestyle to achieve salvation. But we are forgiven and restored to
our heavenly Father by faith – not by what we do.

Jesus' death on the cross shows us the extent of God's love for us, and his
willingness to forgive us. 'We have then, brothers, complete freedom to go
into the Most Holy Place by means of the death of Jesus.'

The song reinforces the message that we are forgiven – not by anything
that we can do – but by his love.

Thieves' Paradise

The sketch takes place in the local pub. The two characters may be supping from beer glasses.

A: It near broke my heart to see old Barney hanging there.

B: Hanging where?

A: On a big wooden cross.

B: So why was he doing that?

A: Well, mostly because of the nails.

B: What, real nails?

A: Yes.

B: That's a bit barbaric. You could kill someone like that.

A: They did. Barney, Jim and that Jesus.

B: So Barney's dead, is he?

A: Yeah, he was crucified.

B: Nasty.

A: He was a good bloke.

B: Well, he wasn't that good – he was a thief. That's why they crucified him, I expect.

A: Yes, but he was a good thief.

B: No, he wasn't. He got caught.

A: He never had any luck.

B: No.

A: Fancy breaking into a geezer's house when you absolutely positively know he's not going to be there, and then being caught in the act when he comes home totally unexpected.

B: Yeah. What was that bloke's name?

A: Lazarus.

B: Chance in a million, that.

A: Yeah. Poor old Barney.

B: Mind you, Jim wasn't much better. I mean, fancy breaking into a house only to find the owner had given everything away.

A: Blooming Zacchaeus.

B: And fancy both of them breaking into that gatekeeper's house. . . .

A: Only to be spotted by an eyewitness.

A and B: Blind Bartimaeus.

A: Still, in their line of work they knew they were taking a risk.

B: What about that other bloke?

A: Who, Jesus?

B: What was his crime?

A: It was funny that. No one seemed to know.

B: What was he? A thief? Con man? Fraudster? Mugger?

A: Rabbi.

B: What, a holy man?

A: Apparently. He had a sign on his cross saying he was the King of the Jews. But I heard people saying that he was the Son of God.

B: If he was the Son of God, what was he doing nailed to a cross?

A: That's what Jim said. He gave him a really hard time, mocking him and shouting at him to save himself and them.

B: Jim was a hard man.

A: As hard as nails.

B: Not quite . . . What about Barney?

A: Barney was a bit different. He seemed to recognise something in Jesus.

B: It's a pity he didn't meet him earlier. He might not have ended up where he did.

A: They seemed to get on well enough, though, given the circumstances.

B: How do you mean?

A: I heard Barney ask if Jesus would remember him when he came into his kingdom.

B: As if Jesus didn't have enough on his plate.

A: That's what I thought. But Jesus made him this promise, see.

B: What kind of promise can you make to a dying man?

A: He said, 'I tell you the truth: today you will be with me in paradise.'

B: What do you think he meant by that?

A: That he was for . . . for . . . for . . .

B: Four sheets to the wind?

A: No, that he was for . . . for . . . for . . .

B: For he's a jolly good fellow?

A: No, that he was for . . . for . . . for . . .

B: Fortunate?

A: Hardly. No, that he was . . . forgiven.

51

B: Oh.

A: Yeah, nice thought that.

B: Anyway, I'm going to miss old Barney.

A: Yeah, but at least his suffering is over.

B: Was that Jesus the same bloke who's been preaching all over the place?

A: I suppose so, yeah.

B: I heard him once.

A: Oh yeah?

B: I hope that when he made him that promise he knew what Barney's profession was.

A: What do you mean? A house breaker? Well, what does that matter now?

B: Because it was Jesus who said, 'In my Father's house are many mansions.'

A: Then Barney really will be in paradise.

FORGIVEN

Paul Field

With a $\frac{12}{8}$ feel

For - giv - en, for - giv - en, for-giv-en by His love. For- giv - en, for - giv - en, for-giv-en by His love. No - thing I do, and no-thing I say can

ev - er be — e - nough.— I'm for - giv - en, for -

Last time to Coda ⊕ (After % only – repeat from %%)

giv - en, for giv - en by His love.
(For -)

Verse

1. How
2. He

eas - il - y we cri - ti - cise,— and try to — pass — the blame;
knows the peo - ple — that we — are,— He knows the — things we — do;—

it's al - ways_ some - one_ els - e's fault, __ a
no mat - ter __ how _ we _ fail, __ His faith-ful_ love_

face to fit __ the _ frame. __
_ is al - ways_ true. __

But Je - sus __ said _ let _ no -
Sur-ren┼dered_to __ the _ cross_

- one _ stand _ a - lone, __
_ that _ we __ might _ live, __

a -

let the one_who's guilt - less throw the stone. __
live a - gain_with pow - er to for - give. __

For -

Forgiven, forgiven, forgiven by his love.
Forgiven, forgiven, forgiven by his love.
Nothing I do and nothing I say can ever be enough:
I'm forgiven, forgiven, forgiven by his love.

How easily we criticise and try to pass the blame;
It's always someone else's fault, a face to fit the frame.
But Jesus said 'Let no one stand alone,
Let the one who's guiltless throw the stone.'

Forgiven, forgiven, forgiven by his love.
Forgiven, forgiven, forgiven by his love.
Nothing I do and nothing I say can ever be enough:
I'm forgiven, forgiven, forgiven by his love.

He knows the people that we are, he knows the things we do;
No matter how we fail, his faithful love is always true.
Surrendered to the cross that we might live,
Alive again with power to forgive.

Forgiven, forgiven, forgiven by his love.
Forgiven, forgiven, forgiven by his love.
Nothing I do and nothing I say can ever be enough:
I'm forgiven, forgiven, forgiven by his love.

Is there life after death?

CONVERSATION STARTER: Do you believe in life after death?

DRAMA: Stephen.

MUSIC: Light a candle in your heart.

The story of Stephen in Acts 7:54-60 graphically shows a Christian who is not afraid of death because he has a wonderful vision of Jesus and an assurance of life eternal. 'Look!' he said. 'I see heaven opened and the Son of Man standing at the right side of God' (Acts 7:56).

As Christians we can face death at any time because we know that after we die we will be in the wonderful presence of our Friend and Saviour for ever.

The assurance of everlasting life brings great joy and helps to put everything in perspective in the struggles of this earthly life.

The song 'Light a candle in your heart' reminds us that:

> Death shall never have dominion
> Where the King of Life shall reign.

Stephen

A: I watched them drag Stephen from the city.

B: They took him to die.

C: Yelling, we stoned him.

A: Screaming, I begged them to stop.

D: Patiently, I waited for it all to be over.

B: I heard him say . . .

C: Look!

A: And he lifted his head.

C: I see heaven open and the Son of Man standing at the right hand of God.

B: We covered our ears against such words.

A: Such a vision!

D: Such blasphemy!

A: Such certainty.

C: So we took him to a place outside the city.

D: There they laid cloaks at my feet.

B: And we took up stones and hurled them.

C: Mine hit him here, on the upper arm.

A: I saw him flinch.

D: Stephen prayed . . .

C: Lord Jesus, receive my spirit.

A: He fell to his knees.

B: Stones rained on him.

A: He cried out . . .

C: Lord, do not hold this sin against them.

A: And then he fell asleep.

B: But I saw it on his face. There was a deeper joy.

C: He showed no fear – although he must have known pain.

D: And later, during my own times of suffering, I remembered his words . . .

C: The Son of Man standing at the right hand of God.

A: He lit a flame of witness, which has been passed on – one to one.

B: He has received the promise of God and it has carried him home.

LIGHT A CANDLE IN YOUR HEART

Paul Field

(1.3.) Light a can-dle in your heart   for the ones who trav-el
          (2.) eyes,   a flame that noth-ing can des -
          (4.)   For the ones who trav-el

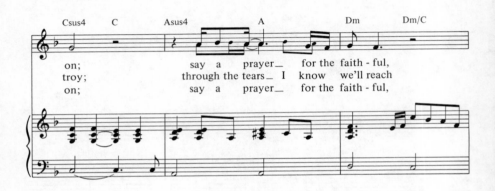

on;   say a prayer_ for the faith - ful,
troy;   through the tears_ I know we'll reach
on;   say a prayer_ for the faith - ful,

still hold - ing on. _2 Light a fire_ with-in_ your
a   deep - er joy..
still hold - ing on._

We play the games of child-hood, ___ we play the mu-sic of ro-mance but it's not un-til ___ the song is ov-er can we real-ly start ___ to dance. ___ It can be hard to say good-bye, _____ it can be hard ___ to un-der-stand, oh,

some-times we don't know ev'-ry ans-wer, but we be-lieve they're safe in the Fa-ther's hands. __ Light a can-dle in your __

And death shall nev-er have dom-in-ion where the King of life __ shall

__ reign; by His Spi-rit, when this life __ is ov-er,

2nd time to Coda ⊕

64

we'll dance to-geth-er a - gain. *(Tacet_____)*

CODA

We'll dance to-geth-er.

Light a can - dle in your heart. *(Slower)*

rall.

65

Light a candle in your heart, for the ones who travel on.
Say a prayer for the faithful, still holding on.
Light a fire within your eyes, a flame that nothing can destroy.
Through the tears I know we'll reach a deeper joy.

We play the games of childhood,
We play the music of romance;
But it's not until the song is over
We can really start to dance.

It can be hard to say goodbye;
It can be hard to understand.
Sometimes we can't know every answer.
But we believe they're safe in the Father's hands.

Light a candle in your heart, for the ones who travel on.
Say a prayer for the faithful, still holding on.

Death shall never have dominion
Where the King of life shall reign.
By his Spirit when this life is over
We'll dance together again.

Light a candle in your heart, for the ones who travel on.
Say a prayer for the faithful, still holding on.
Light a fire within your eyes, a flame that nothing can destroy.
Through the tears I know we'll reach a deeper joy.

Death shall never have dominion
Where the King of life shall reign.
By his Spirit when this life is over
We'll dance together again.

Light a candle in your heart.

BURNING QUESTION 8

Can I know Jesus?

The core of the Christian experience is a relationship with the living Jesus Christ. Countless millions of Christians around the world know him as a personal and living Friend.

When Saul of Tarsus set out to destroy the church, and to persuade the early believers to forsake their risen Saviour he had a dramatic experience on his way to Damascus (Acts 9:1-19). He heard a voice calling, 'Saul, Saul! Why do you persecute me?' This was the turning point in his life, transforming him from being a persecutor of Christians to one of the greatest missionaries that the church has ever known.

The start of the Christian life is the start of a pilgrimage with Jesus. There may be nothing particularly dramatic or emotional about the first steps on this journey . . . but they can lead on to a friendship with Jesus which is one of the richest experiences life has to offer.

The song 'Burning Questions' tells everyone:

> There's nothing now can hurt you,
> It's love that brings you here.

When we discover Jesus then we begin to find the answers to the burning questions in our hearts.

Spies R Us

This sketch has five speaking parts and scope for any number of additional Mr X's.

SPY 1: *[Enters and knocks on a door. The door is opened by a woman.]* The pickled cow is already blue.

WOMAN: What?

SPY 1: The pickled cow is already blue.

WOMAN: If you say so, dear. But I think you've got the wrong address.

SPY 1: Oh. I'm looking for the Spies and Undercover Guild – Jerusalem Chapter.

WOMAN: Oh them! They're meeting next door. Another secret get-together, is it?

SPY 1: Yes . . . I mean no. I mean maybe.

WOMAN: Well, you just tell them to keep the noise down this time. These walls are paper thin.

SPY 1: Right. Ta. I mean thank you. *[He knocks on another door. The door is opened by* SPY 2.*]* The pickled cow is already blue.

SPY 2: And the red herring is best eaten with custard.

SPY 1: Thank goodness!

SPY 2: Quick, come in. We don't want the neighbours to suspect anything.

SPY 1: No, of course not.

SPY 2: Let me introduce you to everyone. I'm Mr X and over there is Mr X. Next to him is Mr X and on his right is Mr X. That's Mr X, Mr X, and Mr X, on the settee. And that's Mr X in the corner.

SPY 1: Where? Behind the potted plant?

SPY 2: No, disguised as the potted plant.

SPY 1: That's amazing.

SPY 2: And your name is?

SPY 1:	Mr X. No relation.
SPY 2:	Good to meet you. Well I think everyone is here now. So, let's get under way. X, could you read the minutes of the last meeting?
SPY 3:	Glib sprottle glob. Mip sly blip mootle mar gleep. Plitch.
SPY 2:	Perhaps you could decode them first?
SPY 3:	Spittle. I mean sorry.
SPY 2:	We'll come back to those later. Now this meeting has been convened to discuss the Nazarene file.
SPY 4:	What, again?
SPY 2:	The matter hasn't been dealt with to anyone's satisfaction as yet.
SPY 4:	How can one carpenter cause so much trouble?
SPY 1:	But I thought he was supposed to be dead.
SPY 2:	He is.
SPY 1:	Then what's the problem?
SPY 2:	He didn't stay that way.
SPY 1:	How can you not stay dead?
SPY 2:	He got better.
SPY 1:	You mean to say he's found a cure for death?
SPY 2:	The evidence does seem to point in that direction, yes.
SPY 4:	Unreasonable behaviour, that's what he's displaying. Rising from the dead. I mean, it's not natural.
SPY 2:	Maybe. But it's not actually illegal either. Inconvenient, yes. Inconsiderate, certainly. But resurrection is not technically an offence. The man's been tried, found guilty, and executed once already. It would be embarrassing to go through it all again. Now, any thoughts on the matter? Yes, X?
SPY 3:	Ten plinkle fitch?
SPY 2:	That's a good point, but I'm afraid there are too many witnesses who have seen him up and about. They can't all be hallucinating.
SPY 1:	You are sure he was actually dead? I mean he might just have been pretending to die.
SPY 2:	I oversaw the execution myself, on behalf of our paymasters, the Sanhedrin. The subject was dead within six hours of being nailed to that cross. It was a neat, professional job.
SPY 4:	Have we made any progress in discovering who this man really was?
SPY 2:	That's the burning question. If we knew who this Jesus

Davidson *really* was we could take the appropriate action.

SPY 1: Supposing he really is the Son of God.

SPY 2: Don't be ridiculous.

SPY 1: Well, that's what people are saying.

SPY 2: Are they indeed?

SPY 1: Yes.

SPY 2: Well, I think it's time we took decisive action. I'm assigning special agent Saul of Tarsus to the case. He'll sort these people out.

SPY 4: He's a bit extreme, isn't he?

SPY 2: He'll get the job done. I can't see him going around letting people say that Jesus is the Son of God. Yes, Saul of Tarsus is the man we need. I know exactly where to send him. Anybody got a map of Damascus?

BURNING QUESTIONS

Paul Field

Steadily
Intro.

Verse

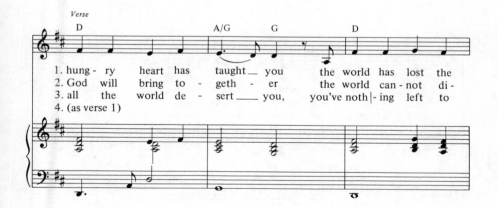

1. hung - ry heart has taught __ you the world has lost the
2. God will bring to - geth - er the world can - not di -
3. all the world de - sert __ you, you've noth |- ing left to
4. (as verse 1)

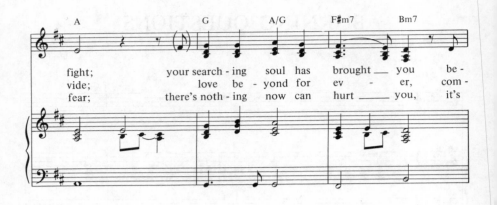

fight; your search-ing soul has brought __ you be-
vide; love be - yond for ev - er, com-
fear; there's noth-ing now can hurt __ you, it's

neath the cross to - night. This sign of love and
pas - sion cru - ci - fied. This sign of death and
love that brings you here. This sign of truth and

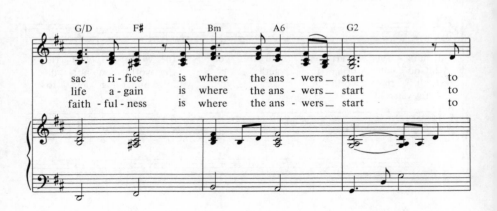

sac ri - fice is where the ans - wers __ start to
life a - gain is where the ans - wers __ start to
faith - ful - ness is where the ans - wers __ start to

ev' - ry burn - ing ques - tion in ____ your heart.
ev' - ry burn - ing ques - tion in ____ your heart.
ev' - ry burn - ing ques - tion in ____ your heart.

2. What
3. Though   In ____ your heart.
4. Your

Your hungry heart has taught you
The world has lost the fight.
Your searching soul has brought you
Beneath the cross tonight.
This sign of love and sacrifice
Is where the answers start
To every burning question in your heart.

What God will bring together
The world cannot divide.
Love beyond for ever,
Compassion crucified.
This sign of death and life again
Is where the answers start
To every burning question in your heart.

Though all the world desert you
You've nothing left to fear.
There's nothing now can hurt you –
It's love that brings you here.
This sign of truth and faithfulness
Is where the answers start
To every burning question in your heart.

ON FIRE

Paul Field

Pen - te - cost, by heav - en come to ___
his - to - y the mes - sage stays the ___

earth. Young men will ___ see vis -
same: glo - ri - fy ___ the Fa -

- ions, old men will ___ dream dreams;
- ther, wit - ness to ___ the Son, ___

___ where God pours out His
___ to burn with His com -

Spi - rit, the work of love __ is seen.
pas - sion un - til the race __ is run. __

On
On

CODA

'till we

are on, 'til we are on

fire. _____

The 'On fire' song

On fire, to carry the flame.
On fire, renew us again.
On fire, to lift up the name of Jesus.
On fire, a light in the land.
On fire, to live hand in hand.
On fire, together we stand,
Till we are on fire.

We celebrate the moment
Of the church's birth
By the flame of Pentecost,
By Heaven come to earth.
Young men will see visions,
Old men will dream dreams;
Where God pours out his Spirit
The work of love is seen.

On fire, to carry the flame.
On fire, renew us again.
On fire, to lift up the name of Jesus.
On fire, a light in the land.
On fire, to live hand in hand.
On fire, together we stand,
Till we are on fire.

Through these days of conflict
In this world of change;
Across the page of history
The message stays the same.
Glorify the Father,
Witness to the Son,
To burn with his compassion until the race is run.

On fire, to carry the flame.
On fire, renew us again.
On fire, to lift up the name of Jesus.
On fire, a light in the land.
On fire, to live hand in hand.
On fire, together we stand,
Till we are on fire.